sonoffred

second edition

poems by

mh clay

Rebel Poetry Ireland

sonoffred

Second Edition ©2024

Published by
REBEL POETRY
Kent Street
Fermoy
County Cork
Ireland

Tel: int + 353 25 30661
www.rebelpoetryireland.com
email:rebelpoetryireland@gmail.com

Cover illustration by Laura de Barry
www.lauradebarra@wordpress.com

ISBN: 979-8-218-42982-9

For Sara

And for Gene
May he rest with the angels

Acknowledgments

Acknowledgements are due to the editors of the following poetry houses where some of these poems have appeared:

Allegiance first appeared on P.A.O's Open Mic Project, www.paoprod.com/Projects/Open-Mic/OpenMic.htm, 2007-02013

108 Auspicious Things first appeared in Perhaps This Rain, 2007-2014, Mad Swirl Press

Leadership and *Little* first appeared on Misty Mountain Review, April 2012, www.misty-mountainreview.blogspot.com/2012/04

Youte, *Marvelous Days* and *Buddha's Teeth* first appeared on Mad Swirl's Poetry Forum, 2009-2014, www.madswirl.com/content/po-etry/m_h_clay.html

Contents

Foreword

I've had the distinct honor of introducing this prolific poet, happy harp blowing, word slinging mad man named MH Clay many times to the stage over the years. I've called this man of many hats (literally!) numerous things to include: poet; artist; editor; musician; confidante; Mad co-conspirator; and my all-time favorite... friend. And even now, after all these years, I am finding that there are many more sides to this soul; known as MH to many, Michael to others, Uncle Mikey to a few, oh, and "son of fred," too.

I began to see a few new glints of him when I first delved into this fine collection of his poetry. Gathered here, between a front and back cover, stacked with rhyming recollections of good times plus a few mad dashes of alliteration, is more than a body of work from MH Clay.

This book might as well be MH, himself. Glimpses and reflections of him as devoted husband, lively lover, role-model father, fine friend and sensitive son can be seen here. He gives us a view from where he was, where he is, and where he is going. As the man himself says, "You can see where I've been from the front my hat" And what places his hat has been! After a few pages you'll see what I mean. I'm not going to say "I hope you enjoy this collection of poetry from MH Clay" because I can say, without a single doubt, that you will.

Johnny Olson
Founder & Chief Editor
Mad Swirl

sonoffred

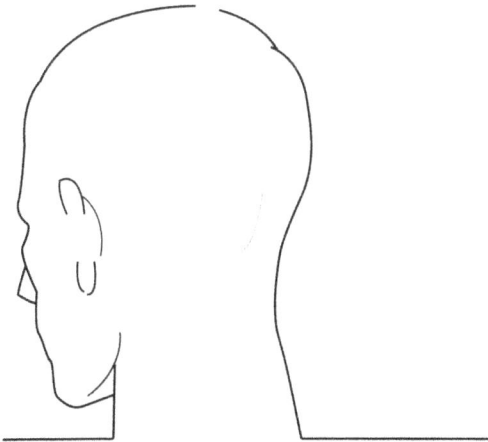

My Old Age

I think of my good fortune
To live this life with you
We take the fun
Embrace the pain
Brave the storms and turn again
Through rainbows gleaming
After rain

To grow together
Roots entwined
Reaching up, branch and spline
By such identity, we're defined
As two who joined
And jointly won't unwind

All around may fall apart
But we can cope
We can be smart
Allow despair no chance, no start
When all around are so disjointed
We must ourselves be so appointed
To act upon this life-lit stage
I see our story page by page
I mean to be a comfort to you
In my old age

To Think

To think
You could have left me
Back when I was hard against the wall
If you had
I would have chalked it up
To the price I had to pay
For heaven

To think
I had no idea what heaven is
But the reality of you
So sweet and warm
I would forsake
For what was never realized

To think
I might now be looking
For another love
Instead of having your devotion
Your acceptance
The joy of your presence
The exhilaration of lively conversation
I have always had with you

To think of what might have been
Instead of what wonderfully is

Well now, that's absurd,
Isn't it?

Forwards Back

I think I'll just wear my hat backwards
Blatantly showing my ins and my outs
I'll walk leaning forward
With purpose – no doubts
All failure analysis
Retrospective and that
I'm tired of rehashing
I'll leave them for my hat
Yes, I think I'll just wear my hat backwards

I think I will just take up dancing
That Gene Kelly, Fred Astaire
Lightness of being
I'll live in a musical
All melody and light
Where I'll move on my tiptoes
A star in the night
With you as my partner
We'll step and we'll glide
My arm 'round your waist
And to hell with my pride
We'll tango and cha-cha
We'll sway and we'll swing
We'll still be responsible
But we'll laugh and we'll sing
Yes, I think I will just take up dancing

I think I'll just start drinking tropical drinks
From glasses with parasols and parrot-shaped swizzlers
With the manner of living

That goes with the drink
The stress free, I-don't-care
I'm-on-vacation type think
This is the way that I'll start to be
I know that this mindset is better for me
Yes, I think I'll just start drinking tropical drinks

So, drinking and dancing
My hat facing back
I'm going to move forward
I'm getting the knack
While dancing and drinking
Occasionally stumbling
There's really no difference
I'm still only bumbling
Through this way and that

You can see where I've been
From the front my hat

Inept Thievery

We share this tropic night
With a gecko
In the glass
Slurping the dregs
Of our hilarity
To flop out
Slip and skitter
Down the crack
Gone

Left behind
This wind, these stars
That moon
And the soft feel
Of your fingertips
As I reach across to you

Bleak and Blue

For Sara

So bleak and blue
So hard for you
To share the weight
Of what we do
All on yourself you take it

And, yes
I, too

Flashback #5

One day you'll get this
One day you'll smile
When you have your own flashbacks
Of precious times

Long ago moments
When you needed my hand
Found security in our rule
Stay close to Dad
When I would walk you
Through the place of the dead
And teach you to see it with wonder
Not dread
I read you the headstones
Who died
What loved ones left behind
What slice of time
Such a strange idea for toddling minds
For whom everything was now

All so now – back then
Do you remember when
We walked on gravel paths?
Your small hands
Tightly gripping mine
Your small eyes
Opened, oh so wide
To take it all in
In the graveyard
In the braveyard
Too young to be on guard

Too new to be threatened
So safe to walk with Dad

How much happier could I be
To know that then
Safe Dad was me

Elbow Room

On my elbow
I'm viewing the corpse of a fly
I'm obliged to forego the post mortem
No time to consider
The larval stages
The struggle to burst free
From the constricts of pupae
It's all just a lot of buzzing around
Regurgitating, so we can eat
Flying and fucking
And laying the eggs
Until all over exhausted
And spirit expelled
We tumble down falling
To light on my elbow
Where I'm viewing the corpse of a fly

The Great Zambini

The Great Zambini
Center stage
The spotlight yellow
Slowly dilates
The red satin of his cape
A fire on his chest
A flourish
The cape is tossed aside
To reveal an upheld, empty
White-gloved hand
Becomes a lotus blossom
The cusp of the grand circle
Life's promenade

    A yellow light comes on
    The afterburner light
    The open door of the chamber
    A hungry, ravenous, glowing mouth
    Waiting to receive
    Saying, *Ahhh!*
    To the morsel
    That is my father

Zambini waves his magic wand
And my father appears
Floating above plush, red carpet
Back-dropped by purple velvet
A white sheet draped over his body
Flowing to the floor
Gravity defied by this levitation act

Oh, my father
I see you now
Silver, auburn hair
Swept back and hanging down
Your face, brown leather
You're not here, I know this
But I cry bitter tears
Because I so want you to be
A little boy am I
Seeking his father's comfort
Father's solid shelter

Zambini speaks, *Presto, Chango!*

My father's body
Encased in white cardboard
Slides off the gurney
Into the gaping maw
The metal teeth clang shut
A red light flashes
"Cremation chamber"
The temperature climbs

Alakazam!
The flashing ruby
On Zambini's turban
Hypnotizes all
I'm entranced
He's there again
Floating in space again
Speaking to me
In stoic, stony silence
I am with you, my son!
I am in you, my son!

Look in the mirror every day
And I'll be staring back at you
Smiling acceptance and approval at you
Shine your shoes
Like I taught you
Look at the reflection
That you see in the toe
I'll be looking in on you, my son!

Throat air, open
Hearth air, dampened
The temperature
Eight, nine hundred,
One thousand degrees F
Ashes are forming

A gray mound of remembrance
A potassium, calcium legacy

The levitation is complete
I stretch out my hand
To touch his chest
Cold beneath the white sheet
I cannot bring myself to touch his cheek, his chin
I say goodbye
He floats upward
Into the ceiling, into the clouds

The Great Zambini
Magic wand in hand
Makes the sign of the cross
The curtain falls
The lights come up
The crowd applauds

Into the night, we pour

I'm walking now
Through the darkness
On the far gray horizon
A line of orange peeks
Confidence whispering in my ear
As I walk into the growing
Yellow-gray glowing
Hopeful, distant
Dawn

In The Crapper

When he crapped on the floor
They scolded and shouted him
Into droop-tailed dejection

When again he crapped on the floor
They added on
They rubbed his nose in it
Then locked him in his cage
For an appropriate period
To whimper in his anguish and remorse; yet,

Still he crapped...

They threw up their hands
They let him go

As he moved from house to house
When he crapped on a floor
They watched in dismay

As he barked at himself
Rubbed his own nose in it
Then crawled into his cage
For an appropriate period
To whimper in his anguish and remorse

He suffered this punishment
To justify his crimes; yet,

Still he crapped

Allegiance

My unconscious allegiance
Was all it took for me to be out of sync
Even though I executed detailed instructions
Like a detailed executioner

With no breach of rule intended
Sometimes I cut the loaf
And others, the breadboard
Until the slice and splinter
Became the bane of me

Protracted exposure to that annealing light
That ever deepest thought revealing light
Made jumping back to edge of night
An ever so appealing sight
When after all
The hand suspended over searing fire
Will soon pull back by reflex

For all that penance and self-inspection
The self one sees in that reflection
With whom to join and be as one
Is the self we have been all along

You in your Che Guevarra T-shirt

You in your Che Guevarra
T-shirt

You don't know
How he's glancing
Off your back
Smugly taunting me
To drink in your virgin beauty

You less-than-twenty-something
Sweetheart
Walking behind you
I could be Daddy
But not Grandpa

And my fantasy says
All things are possible

Youte

Anse La Ray, St. Lucia
A Friday night in June, 2002

Sick Youte!
Wicked Youte!
Say the shopkeepers

Through these streets
Youte runs
Youte of the Friday nights
Youte of the street parties
The islanders move late
Move into the night

In the disco, lights are flashing
Rastas groove to the reggae, country beat
Vacillating, syncopating
Rhythm and color spill into the street

Where sounds and smells
Attack the senses
Lobster, shrimp, seafood all
Life is consumed here
In great, gulping mouthfuls

There stands Augustine Raspar
Spouting wisdom for any to hear
I make everyone dance!
He laughs, *Because you never know.*
So, live fast and quit!
Amen

There stands the church
Graveyard full of those who danced
Youte grins a skeleton grin
He towers far above the town
Grinning down
Below him, pulsing mad and fast
Rastas, lobsters, island women
Sleek and brown
White-skinned tourists

The music rises
Engulfing all in a flood
Youte moves through the crowd
Taps each reveler on the shoulder
To lead a long conga line
Down to the shore
Skeleton grin
Until everyone is smiling

Say the shopkeepers,
Sick Youte!
Wicked Youte!

Proxy

To express out loud our deep desires
From soul to page to spoken word
I would last
I would see all

To be specially cursed for speaking so
For giving life to that word
That burgeons deep inside us all
And in speaking out
To be condemned
When we all sit at sea sides
To seize the view
To grab on, hold tight

Hear my voice
My puppet mouth
I am happily duped to do the job
When such thought grows
In the visceral host
There is no more inevitable event

The word *will* find a mouth
And make dupes of those
Who feared to give it voice

Immortality

In the garden
A lone blossom
A magenta mandala
Spinning round a bright white core
An infinite center

In the parlor
Sweet sounds of forgiveness
Sung from a common soul

There are no boundaries
No borders
No inability to feel the same
We are together
Expressing a common love

This is our ground
Our mutual heart, our home
There is no distance
Nothing too far

On the table
A flame pulses on the glass
The wine waltzes with the light
A soft red light to warm us all

The magenta bloom
Not a barrier, but a door
A portal to this eternal moment
This moment we hold
This moment we covet
Together

Why would God
Begrudge us this?

Détente

Man! I saw god!
He was wearing
A pin-striped suit
And he called me
Ron!

I was pioneering
Unfurrowed ground
Seeds scattered
Unfound

Who knows what shoots
Spurt up through loam
To stretch up tall?
What winding roots
Will rise and question
Flight from fall?
What's in a name,
Big Guy?

What indeed?
What sky?
What clown
Can lighten smile
From frown?

What blue?
What, god, is troubling you?
Not me, surely

Not we, who turn left
From right?

Call me Ron
Or Don
Or John o' the Cross
No matter what name

No harm
No loss

Airplane

Little Sarah
The tippy-toe queen
Enthroned in her chlorine blue
Aquatic cocoon
She is hibernating there
She's a chrysalis
Awaiting metamorphosis

Head back, chin up
She is suspended
Arms straight out, fingers waving
Taking in the changing light
The bobbing surface
Reflecting her, now large, now small
With each undulation
She vibrates in her amniotic goo

Me standing, back to the sun
Gazing down on such delight
On little Sarah, oozing light
And looking so intently through me
Through my chest, through my eyes
Onward, up to deep blue skies

Airplane! she says
She imitates, arms still outstretched
Shimmering in her chlorine stew
She flew

It's my airplane!

Naked Surprise

In this delightful paradise
The greatest storm we'll weather
Is likely to be the decision
Over what we'll have for dinner
We agreed to roll the vacation dice
And do this all together
To cohabit without derision
No need to judge, no guilty sinners

But now there's the matter of the pool
That cool oasis down the hill
And what ideas we start to thinking
Especially on a night of drinking
When amorous intentions spill
And each, not prepared to be the fool
Has desires to, in the night, go tripping
But won't realize
The awkward surprise
That will come from not scheduling
The skinny dipping

My Addiction

I'm in the soup
Stirred up and moving to
The vibe in this place
Feeling such an up-charge

But soon, I'm seeing
My addiction
Crouched in the corner
Leering at me
He wants me to see him
As large as the room
Wants me to let him
Take over

His earnest gaze
Convinces me that he knows
I know I can see him
Watching my addiction watch me

My sick seducer inspires me now
Discomfort induced by him
Propels me
To establish new perimeters
Defy old boundaries

I can see my addiction
Crippled by my indifference
Shrinking
Paralyzed by my light

Which lights this scene
Of mine
Watching my addiction watch me

Puzzle Box

For Isaac

Head back, eyes closed
Brow knit, tongue twixt teeth
Working the panels
Guessing the sequence
So consumed in sleuthing
The contents are not the point

Opening the box
Solving the puzzle
That's the objective
That's the goal

We learned early
This box holds treasure
Not seen by man
We heard it can be opened
But never has
So, one and all
We took the dare
Open it we shall

Groping now, pushing
Eyebrows joined, lips pursed white
We strain our ears
To hear that soft *click*
The sound that tells us
Now we can open
Now we can see

Sitting at our small table
In our bare room
We see the box open
With the lid laid back
To reveal, inside
In miniature
Our several selves
Heads back, eyes closed
Brows knit, tongues twixt teeth
Working little puzzle boxes

All Night Lanes

At the Balcony Club, 12 Nov 06

Blue embroidered, above the heart
Butch and *Barry* and *Killer* and *Glen*
Green and red striped, smooth-soled shoes
So's not to scratch the sacred wood
Reducing friction for the incense ball
That rolls and sanctifies
From narthex to altar
Knocks down the boys
A righteous strike
Extra points for the poor
10 lanes, open all night
Where confession's best
When you go to the restroom
To pee back holy water
Look in the mirror to ask forgiveness
While outside the door
The background rumble of falling pins
Is the voice of God
Pronouncing penances
It's team competition tonight
And ladies drink free!

Destiny Loop

Destiny had a fit of indigestion
    The pattern of multitude lives perhaps backed up
Too much to process
I caused a reflex regurgitation
And was belched out
Dropped out of the loop

Suddenly, the circumstances of life
Have no real significance
They don't add up in a grand tally
There will be no celestial diploma
With all my triumphs and trials
Scribed in letters of gold
    My ticket to the joys thereafter

Out of the loop
The car broke down
Just because it did
The job was lost
Just because it was
My life goes on
Just because it does
I can make whatever I like of it
Or make it nothing at all

But, out of the loop
Cause and effect still hold
Action still begs reaction

I must be wise
Must learn
Keep moving
Until one day, maybe
When Destiny inhales deeply   abruptly
As if to stifle a sneeze
And sucks me back into the loop

Marvelous Days

Mundane, yet marvelous
These days, these hours
These distasteful diversions
They, too, have taste to
Broaden the palate
Bring each day to light
To linger on the tongue

Learning is limned
In my luminous limitations
These shackles adorn me
Then, cold splash, face slap
They warn me -
Alive be, awake!
Should the night
My soul to take

Quotidian quiescence
Stupefies
Effort's required
To open sleepy eyes
The day is bright
The hours ahead, right

These are marvelous days

Blue Sky

Above you
Such a blue, blue sky
A celestial height
A turquoise vault
Underneath
The grand parade
With a marching band
And the Holiday Queen
So beautiful and kind

You join the great procession
The grand promenade
Your blessed Queen leads the way
The crowd parts in adoration and awe

Now upward
You ascend
Into that blue, blue sky
Higher, until curling clouds
Caress your feet

The azure air
So cold and crisp
Below you now
Before you,
Only stars and stars and stars
You strain to see yourself in their weak light
To feel some slight touch of their wan warmth
Across the vast and endless void

Around you
There is black, black, black
Beyond the blue, blue sky

At the Absinthe Lounge

Thanks to Kevin

Smoke that thing
Bing, smoke it hard
Blow your be-bop passed the doors
Where we all checked our guards
Pop it out sharp
Sharp as a pin
Pick out the riffs of this place we're in
So long as we're generous with the gin

Flash those lights in our faces
Ace, take us to those
Yellow, red and blue places
Drill'em out, drop those notes in order
Draw out this moment
Into longer and shorter
And sooner or later
You'll all know where you've been
So long as we're generous with the gin

Hold that final chord, Ward
Sustained and pulsing in our heads
Ripple sound to hold us still
Close to overflow our fill
Just this side of fears and dreads
You'll meet a sweeter lord
Above propriety and sin
So long as we're generous with the gin

36

Stradivariuses Sequenced

Slab-bottomed stew pot
Surface seething
Bubbling breathing
Vaporizing vivid effervescence
Freedom flock flapping
Fluttering cluttering
Cloud-free sky
With emancipated entities
Skittering by

Dodging the down-hammer dredge
Shattering surfaces
Insufficiently scattered
With shimmering shields
And blow-glancing scales
Unnatural outgrowths
From slamming the slew
Sledge and stammer
No less for the noise
Coming back at you

Master that tremolo
Finger and twist
The hum of the soul
The twitch of the wrist

José

I should have gotten to know
José Ascencion
How cool he was
Last chair in the woodwinds line Playing a baritone sax
Tall as he
Stretching his arm
Chin lifting up to hold his lips
To the reed
Like some Seuss-concocted
Little Whoville tooter
Blasting on a megalophonium
Big as a house

He had to have courage
And a sense of humor
Just squeezin' out notes
To keep the elephant god
From sneezin' his home away

José, my man, we could have been friends!
I'm sorry I had my adolescent head
Shoved so far up my
    Gotta walk cool cuz everyone's watchin'
    Hours lookin' at the back of my noggin
    With a mirror and a comb
    Cuz that back-part was the first thing
    That anyone would see
Jr. High Band
Candy ass

Childish Things

We look at the world once, in childhood.
The rest is memory.
—Louise Gluck

I look out this window
To see my father coming up the back walk
Whistling beneath the poplar tree
Whistling *Glow, Little Glow Worm*
Then I know all is well with him
Therefore well with me

Someone told me I should fear God
As I feared Fred
And fear him I did
Gulping down dread
Stuck in my guilty dry throat
Terrified by the switch
The endless hang-time horrible moment
Between the swing and the swat
The painful searing relief
Which came with knowing I had paid
But, when Fred would whistle
And wrap his knuckles on the tabletop
Snapping out rhythms which resonated forgiveness
He assuaged my fear with happiness

But then, I approached the task at hand
Began to act on all that schooling
Stood on adolescent tiptoes
Fists firmly gripping the rising rail

Straining to be bigger, older, better
Yes, I believed that older was better
By the mere living of years
Wisdom would be granted
My sage's service stripes
Would demand subservience
And subordinate salutes

So stupid

I had grabbed for arrogance
And filled my pockets
With other people's purpose

One day, I dropped them
Those hot potato things
Those moldering treasures
Accomplishment, ruthless gloating
This is mine, I don't give a damn for yours

I turned them inside out
To make room for those childish things
Made all the space I could
And shut out the cries

It's a hard world! You gotta be hard!
You must control! You cannot fail!
There's no end, no payment is enough!
Grow up, accept it . . .
Rock on rock, clicking, clacking
Just to make sand
I turned it down, turned it off, turned away
I'm taking hold of old things now

Filling up with hope and confidence
Saving laughter and love

While listening
To hear my father's whistling

Snatch

The grand snatch
That covert creeping blur of flesh
Comes from under the tablecloth
Grabbing greedily the apple pie
Presto chango
There a beat ago
Now gone to sate the surreptitious
Salivating appetite
That lurks beneath the table
Sweet surly snatch

That bite so good so sinfully good
No returning that
When devoured to the core
And reaching again to commandeer more
With those crumbs on the lips
And that glint in the eye
With a shit-eating grin
You can curse God and die
With flexing fearful fingers
You snatch and snatch
Your ecstatic elastic ennui
Outshines the wrath you'll catch

So you snatch and snatch and snatch

Everything Else

You can carry
Your transgressions
Like a mail pouch on your back

Deliver them
To those you think would judge you

All your explanations
Your guilt and your angst,
By not one word
Will they be read
Nor comprehended

Nobody cares
No one notices
Preoccupied they are
With the weight of their own

We shoulder these burdens
Because we think we must
We suffer the blisters
The heat and the dust
Because we are convinced
Someone is keeping score
Every detail recorded
Every foible and more –
    The puny motivations
    Of our selfish souls
    Our ineffective attempts
    To fill our gaping holes

When no one sees those
Bleeding cracks
But us
In our perpetual mirrors
Reflecting always
Into our eyes only

Turn away
Blink twice

Let your tears
Wash away those scales
Shatter the mirror
Into countless shards

See through yourself
To everything else

Picasso Nights

On a night like this
There's always that moment
Full of art and gin
And the company of good friends
When you walk on your cloud
Momentarily distracted
By the need of your bladder
And the clear of your mind

Where you stumble into
A noxious miasma
A volatile plasma reeking stench
To burn nostril hairs
Because somebody chose
Scant moments before
To take a raging rancid chili
Sour beer
Dump

Hammurabi

Go Hammurabi
Lay down your law
As we build your tower
Hold you in awe
While we feed your power
You're the most splendid being
That we ever saw
Hammurabi

You brought us together
With a common tongue
And fountain of life
To keep us young
Yours is the song
We've always sung

Go Hammurabi, teach us truth
Unfold the mysteries of our youth
Lead us on this journey
Through our days
Flatten the mountains
Straighten the ways

Give us strength
Hammurabi
Life of length
Hammurabi

Lines of wisdom
Wizened beard
Smiling down our deepest fears
We follow you, we swallow you
We eat your frame, bear your name
To share your fame
Hammurabi

Singapore Rules

You think you got the high card, big boy?
Think again
There's a hierarchy of suits
And colors and numbers
With a sequence to those
And connectivity
With the fastest influx of info
You listen and learn
To play the card that wins the round

The winning strategy
Hold the king to drop a heart on a diamond
Watch out for a joker or a spade
But, if you knew what you were doing
You would never have sat at the table
The stakes are higher than you can breathe
And breathing is more important
Than winning
When you suffocate for stretching your neck
To see the other guy's ace
And die for wondering
Why he doesn't play it

Jesus in Dallas

Tonight I saw Jesus in Dallas
He was standing on a corner in Deep Ellum
A tall blonde fellow wearing a dark blue pullover
With red and white stripes across the chest and biceps
I think the blue stood for the heavens
The white for purity
And the red for his shed blood

But he wasn't bleeding on the corner
He was standing there with his friends
    They must have been his apostles
They carried big thick bibles under their arms
Like porterhouse steaks
To wave at passing cars
While shouting slogans
One of them wore a sweeping, black leather coat
And a black shirt, buttoned at the collar
With a silver cross around his neck
He might have been Peter, or John

Jesus was holding a large white cross
    Almost as tall as he
Sometimes he balanced it on the sidewalk
Leaning on the cross piece
Or he held it on his shoulder
Holding onto the base
Kind of hugging it
Or, if he got tired,
He leaned it against the brick wall of the building
On the corner where they stood
Now he's holding it again

And Peter, or John, is making grand gestures
    To the passing cars
And clearly saying something great
About Jesus

He really does get around

Jesus in Dallas

Free Fall

(300 meters)

Suspend the fear
Of unexplored experience
Step off the precipice

Four and a half seconds
To float in the ether
Rush of air roaring
Reeling spinning still
'Til taught cord draws tightly
Angels recede to the heavens
Treetops come into view

Leaves flutter
In my sun-soaked breeze
Green yellow glitters
To spell out god's little message,

Welcome back!
Whaddaya think o' reality now?

Leadership

Only the torn ones
    Those who struggle in the mind
Will take the lead

Those who pass from white to black
Endeavoring to hover in the gray
Who venture to step out
Straight into that which black conceals
Where feet may hold or quickly slip away

The timid will follow
Would rather hold back
    Not walk into unknown cold
Would have the warming light against their backs
And move in steps that others took before
Some guarantee of comfort must avail

But the conflicted
Each step they take
Each passing place
Brings questions;
    what changes would have made
    what other paths might have pulled
    what implications of each choice
    what love to keep
    which pain to bear
Or doubt to ponder

To weigh the reason
Left   or   right
Which always must abandon one
To take the other

Especially the one that questions
Whether we were meant
To walk into the light instead

Portuguese Verses

Pen in hand
Empty page
Nothing happening
Apparently
My muse is vacationing, too
Stretched out on these sands
Serenaded by these waves
She is dreaming

Though she bathes topless
In these rays of sun
My compulsion
To reach over
And squeeze a brown nipple
Is not by invitation
I have tried this before
Only to have my hand slapped away

I refrain,
My eager desires restrained
I distract myself instead
Watching a brown man
With gnarled
Tree-root feet
Walking a white dog
With three black spots
And one blue eye

Buddha's Teeth

The Buddha smiles
Thirty-two pearlies
Gleaming white

He is so far beyond
We cannot see
Such blinding light

An ancient princess
Set in motion
The obvious outcome
Of her devotion

So drawn to him
So captivated
His teeth
She prestidigitated

And placed within
A holy shrine
A silver door
She locked behind

The faithful come
The stone is polished
By devoted knees

The chants resound
Entreating Buddha
Nirvana, please!

Buddha had a great idea
Just change the way you think
He said

His misguided followers
Made him into
God instead

Years went on
The message changed
The great idea
Was rearranged

How odd to see
It's not the same
Marred by our
Whisper 'round the circle game

And so it goes
The Buddha muses
When all is one
Nobody loses

Think or pray
The wheel will turn
All the while

Gleaming white
Thirty-two pearlies
Buddha smiles

Seduction

Sidle up to me, sweet siren
And run the risk
Of your dissipation and ruin
Washed in the wastrel verbiage
And verbose vomitus
Of my toxic charm
Touch me and die
Such sweet death as you will never know

For you never go there
Never thought to beware
Of such seduction
So good so deep
The burgeoning bubble
Infuses your empty
Unrealized dreams
With determination and vision
Devoid of vitriolic defeat

Gamble to gain

Channeling Morrison

You tell me you're channeling Jim Morrison
Well, bless his marble slab, aren't we all!
These waves of light
Of sound and sight
Envelope us, shape and develop us
We can bob and sway
And come what may
We snake the lizard through the night
Channeling

Shake it up
Throw it down and break it up
Pour it out in sparkling bits
Sort it out in starts and fits
Smooth it down to a polished glow
'Til reflections of the room we're in
Imitate our collective grin
To captivate us
Engage and fixate us
Preoccupied with watching our own show
Where we need to talk about channeling

Sitting on couches, glasses of wine
Sharing deep feelings
Drawing bold lines
While onion skin peelings expose layer after layer
Where, with irritated tears
We subjugate our fears to laughter and group prayer
We hold on tight
To steady our reeling
With stiff-armed attempts

To fend off the ceiling
Where, wind-blown and unkempt
Our cinema spectacle mirror ball reflection
Of movements and colors commands our attention
Challenges retention of memory, knowledge, bonds
with others
Our group rejection of all that smothers
Our need to make the lizard to snake
To undulate from hip to chin
Our whip-tailed fate of the life we're in
Watching our living
While living our watching
We chase the horizon
Channeling Jim Morrison

Pow Pow

Pull it tight, Boys!
Wind me off
Another notch
Another tooth in the gear
Speak sprocket prophet
Fractious flange, forsooth
Come near

Shut it down, Boys!
Snap my lid
Turn my lock
Another tumbler drop in place
Block the sound
Of prickling lips which
Would pronounce my fate

Pump it up, Boys!
Fill it full
Pack it to popping
With every pull
Every laugh and every smile
Press me out to clarity
Stroking all the while

Pick and strum
Hem and hum
Beat a drum
Pow pow
Pow pow

I would write something happy

Something hopeful and gay
Forsake this monotonous mad meshing of words
My silly stack of syllables
As always, the same thing to say
I dare myself to deviate
Confuse the pattern,   break away
Stop rhyme, drop meter
Abandon this search for words to rhyme with
Angst
No thanks!

Stop whining and pining
For some great idea
Not yet described,
   Ad nauseum, I've tried
Achieving nothing

Stop using
Grand
Sublime, Divine
Useless, Nameless, Void
So many times with words like these
Myself, and others, I've annoyed

Grow up, move on
Pick some new, like
Funny
Ordinary, Deserving, Warm
OK! Hot Dog! Gee Whiz!
Sweet

They don't have to be big
Profound or neat
Days and nights don't have to be tragic
They can be magic
No struggle, no pain
Lived without strain

Let life be
Let go the drama
The spot light, approval, trauma
No matter who watches
Who listens, who scoffs
Who smiles or frowns
Who sneezes or coughs

It's not me
It's not my words
Will make it so

Stars We Are

Trees on a planet
Pins on a cushion
Standing out, little silver soldiers
With tiny helmets to glint the light
Of a red and yellow blazing sun
Casting long, straight shadows
Curved along the face of this sphere

Cross-hatched shadows
Meshing true
Interconnected lines of life
We stand together
We stand alone
Looking straight up
Into a spinning galaxy of stars

Which stars we are

108 Auspicious Things

The golden boy with dreamy gaze
And lazy smile, a secret grin
Attuned to the clinking
Of 108 coins
Metallically tinking in a melodic signature
Only the golden boy understands

Divine music
Which he manipulates from our unconscious
Mortal hands
His lordly lullaby
We pay for his pleasure a thousand times a day
108 rings, repeating, repeating

On the soles of his feet
108 auspicious things
With twenty-seven celestial bodies
Turning, spiraling mandalas
Peepholes to a frightening glimpse
Of this huge universe
Impervious to human control

Should those grand feet
Touch common earth
And the golden boy take a stand
Our material world and puny existence
Would disappear
Sucked through those cosmic holes
On the soles of his feet

So long reclined upon his side
Growing by decades
Expanding by centuries
Becoming as big as the stars
Blinking through the windows in his feet
Hypnotized in his meditative state
Unaware of the roof and the walls
Which imprison him

Outsmarted by the monks
Who built this house
To see that he would never rise
Who reverently offer 108 coins
Infinitely plinking, forever placating
Reverberating days by years by lifetimes
To ensure this world we love endures
So long as those terrifying feet
Never touch the ground

Star Shot

Quick,
Wake the kids!
Have them out to crawl into our laps
Together with our upturned heads
Gaze into the smiling face
Of our imminent demise

Brief streaks of story
Flash across this midnight sky
Our light legacy
Legends told
Heroes bold
Memories recounted
Whole lives unfold
In a wink of frenetic photons

Here and gone
But not forgotten
Our fixed fascination
Ensures a long half-life
For the line
Cycles will come and go
But, meantime
We revel in this show

Look up there, kids!
That short flare
Can flame forever
When we see that
Now never ends

Little

We are little men
Standing small
Against our massive concrete sprawl
Little lives
Lived in turn
But little matter to the Great Big

Little ideas
Little words
Piece them together
Little grunts and gasps
To make a big noise
To be a little big

But still little
Little time to be here
Little years to be noticed
Is no little thing to bear

On the way out
Have a little fun
Exit with a little laugh

About the Poet

MH Clay is a poet, playwright, musician, actor, and raconteur living in Dallas, Texas. Since 2009, he has been Poetry Editor of MadSwirl.com and is co-host of Mad Swirl's Open Mic, held every first Wednesday of the month in Dallas. His publication credits include *ANGST* (Mad Swirl Press 2016); *sonoffred* (Rebel Poetry Ireland, 2015/2024), and *Perhaps This Rain and other precipitations* (2007). His play *Dorian's Uptown Diner* was adapted for screen in 2017, titled *Nighthawks*, by Praxedis Pictures.

He has been a thrice-featured poet at the Blackwater International Poetry Festival in Ireland, 2013, 2014, & 2016, as well as a panelist at Poetry International Rotterdam, 2015, and has been an active member of the Dallas literary community for over two decades.

www.ingramcontent.com/pod-product-compliance
Lightning Source LLC
Chambersburg PA
CBHW070010100426
42741CB00012B/3182